Hi my name is Kate.
I would love to tell you all about my hidden treasure.

But first,
I would love for you to meet my family.
I live with my mother, Lin, my father, John,
big sister, Lisa and little brother, Mike.

1

Kate is awake and remembers the dream she had last night.
She couldn't wait to get dressed.
Kate washed her face.
She brushed her teeth, and put on her clothes.

Kate's mom, Lin, combs and brushes her hair.
She tied two pretty white ribbons with big red polka dots
on each ponytail.
Kate loved it and was now ready for the day.

Kate still had the dream that she had on her mind.
Hidden Treasure!
Kate began to tell her family about the dream.

Kate met up with a few of her friends.
They all began to play lots of games. During one of the
games, Kate realized she had lost one of her pretty, red
polka dot white ribbons.

5

Kate and her friends became tired while looking for
her ribbon, which made her very sad.
They decided to go and get something to eat.

Hot dogs, cotton candy, popcorn,
candy apples, and ice cream.
Kate mom, Lin, had layed out a blanket
early that day.

6

Kate and her friends decided to lay on the blanket
under a big apple tree.

Kate looked up at the apples on the tree, which
reminded her of the big polka dots on her white
ribbon that was in her hair.
Kate happened to drift off to sleep
under the big, red apple tree.

7

She began to dream that she had came back home.
Kate began to climb up the stairs to her room.

She reached out to open the door knob.
Kate notice that the door knob was different.
It was a round crystal with colorful, sparklings diamonds.

Kate opened the door.
The room was like a maze with big, long candy
canes and round peppermint sticks.

9

Kate began to walk through the maze.
Towards the end of the maze was another door.

Kate opened the door.
She saw a gold key floating in the air.

The key fell out of my hands.
I looked for the key everywhere:
under the box's, under the shoes, and
under the clothes.
Where did the it go?

11

Back in the corner of the closet I saw a box.
It was so beautiful with all kinds of colorful stones.

All I could think about was the hidden treasures
inside, and I had found it.
Beautiful! Beautiful!
Beautiful, but where is the key?

12

Kate took the key and began to unlock the beautiful box.
When Kate open the box, she was more amazed.
Inside was another pretty gold key with the name Kate
engraved into it.
A picture of her family, which she loved dearly.

13

Wow!
The pretty white ribbon with the big red polka dots
was also in the treasure box.

Kate began to smile.
She had everything that she needed:
Her family, her pretty ribbon with the big red polka
dots, and the key to her hidden treasure.

The End

14

www.ingramcontent.com/pod-product-compliance
Lightning Source LLC
Chambersburg PA
CBHW040039240726
48664CB00003B/987